LEARNING
I·D·E·A·S
THROUGH THE YEAR

by Sidney Martin and Dana McMillan

illustrated by Corbin Hillam

Related books from The Learning Exchange, Inc.: *Brain Boosters, More Brain Boosters, Science Boosters, Language Boosters.*

Publisher: Roberta Suid
Editor: Carol Whiteley
Production: Susan Pinkerton

Entire contents copyright © 1989 by Monday Morning Books, Inc., Box 1680, Palo Alto, California 94302

Monday Morning is a registered trademark of Monday Morning Books, Inc.

Permission is hereby granted to the individual purchaser to reproduce student materials in this book for non-commercial individual or classroom use only. Permission is not granted for school-wide, or system-wide, reproduction of materials.

ISBN 0-912107-91-X

Printed in the United States of America

9 8 7 6 5 4 3 2 1

Contents

Introduction — 5

Part I. Starting Off Right

Chapter 1. Back to School
Find the Gingerbread Man — 9
What's My Line? — 11
Big Loony Bird — 12
Library Book Maze — 13
All-Star Production — 16
Our Classroom Rules — 18
Bus Riders' Chart — 19
What's Cookin'? — 21
Check It Off — 22

Chapter 2. New Classmates
The Friendship Circle — 23
Big Initials — 24
Cinderella — 25
Meet Your Match — 26
Interview the Celebrities — 27
Scavenger Hunt — 28
Getting to Know You — 30
Circle Name Game — 31
Photo Magic — 32
Welcome to the Bunch — 33
Welcome to the School — 35

Chapter 3. Teamwork and Self-Esteem
Partner Portraits — 37
Look Who's Here Today! — 38
It's My Bag — 39
How Do You Fit In? — 40
Name Tag Jigsaw Puzzle — 42
Kids On Display — 43
My Own Number Chart — 44
Photo Poems — 45
Our Star This Week — 46

Part II. Moving Along

Chapter 4. Sponge (In-Between-Times) Activities
Brainy Lineups — 49
Alphabet Sense — 50
Calendar Capers — 51
Find Your Partner — 52
Riddle Bucket — 53
Word Fun — 54
Hink-Pinks — 55
Silent Math Practice — 56
Sign Punctuation — 57
Guess the Number — 58

Chapter 5. Games for Review
Let's Look at the Facts 59
Let's Trade Questions 60
You Are the Teacher 61
Team Success 62
Spin It 63
Dueling Math Review 64
Fraction Pizza 65
Send Word Home 66

Chapter 6. Thinking Games
Verbs Galore 67
Conversations 68
Making Connections 69
Monday Memories 70
The Great Divide 71
Vocabulary Helper 72
Glob It Up 74

Chapter 7. Cabin Fever Games
Guess Who's Missing 75
Four Corners 76
Get It Together 77
Nursery Rhyme Match-up 78
Addition Relay 79
Drawing Relay 80
Moving North 81
Beanbag Drop 82
World Traveler 83
Signs on Students 84

Part III. Ending with a Bang

Chapter 8. Special Interest Days
Dad's Doughnut Day 87
Rainbow Week 90
Guesstimation Day 93
Personalized Learning Day 95

Chapter 9. The Great Outdoors
Walk A Mile 97
Odd or Even? 98
Firefighter Relays 99
Balloon Float 100
Peanut Pick-up 101
Scatter Ball 102
Fall Out 103
The Shocker 104

Chapter 10. Parting Company
Dinosaur Egg Picnic 105
Picnic Treasure Hunt 106
Exposition Day 110
Your Afternoon Plan 111
It's the Last Day! 112

INTRODUCTION

Teachers sharing with teachers is the brainstorm behind *Learning Ideas Through the Year*. Here is a compilation of successful, classroom-tested ideas from teachers who have participated in the programs of the Learning Exchange, Inc., a nonprofit educational resource center.

The activities in this book are designed to provide you with interesting, involving, interactive projects, grouped according to the seasons of the year. In each section you'll find easy-to-do games, bulletin board ideas, projects, and other creative activities that require little or no preparation or materials.

The beginning-of-the-year section—"Starting Off Right"—includes ideas to help you introduce your students to the school and staff, ways to meet and get to know new classmates, and activities that will help establish a winning team spirit. For example, "How Do You Fit In?" welcomes your new students by asking them to create a class puzzle.

The middle-of-the-year section—"Moving Along"—can provide the spark for your mid-year curriculum. This section includes a chapter of sponge activities designed to fill small periods of time with meaningful yet enjoyable skill review. If cabin fever strikes, "Cabin Fever Games" will give your students a break from sitting without leaving the room.

The end-of-the-year section—"Ending with a Bang"—provides you with ideas for special interest days. This section describes possibilities for organizing your classroom or the entire school around topics both students and teachers will find interesting. There are ideas galore for making the end of the year a time your students will remember.

Through its sixteen years, The Learning Exchange has offered workshops and networking opportunities for educators. *Learning Ideas Through the Year* would not have been possible without those dedicated teachers who were willing to meet with us after their school day to share their best teaching ideas.

       Sidney Martin and Dana McMillan
       The Learning Exchange, Inc.
       2720 Walnut
       Kansas City, MO 64108

The Learning Exchange is a not-for-profit educational resource center. Its staff members and consultants are dedicated to the goal of improving the quality of education by working with teachers to improve the quality of instruction. The Learning Exchange establishes partnerships with the business and educational communities to achieve this goal.

IN APPRECIATION

The Learning Exchange gratefully acknowledges the following educators for the ideas they contributed to this book:

Melanie Caywood
Pam Davison
Leora Jimenez
Sandy Porter
Phyllis Renshaw
Belinda Stephenson
Karen Wilson

The Learning Exchange, Inc.
2720 Walnut
Kansas City, Missouri 64108

PART I
Starting Off Right

CHAPTER 1
Back to School

FIND THE GINGERBREAD MAN

This activity helps introduce students to the school staff and facility.

MATERIALS:
Copy of *The Gingerbread Man* book, copy of the gingerbread man pattern, large sheet of cardboard, markers, colored paper, scissors, glue

DIRECTIONS:
Use the materials to make a large cardboard gingerbread man. On the first day of school, read *The Gingerbread Man* to the class. After reading the story, introduce the cardboard gingerbread man to the class. Remind the students that he will "run as fast as he can" and appear each day in a different spot in the school. Each morning, place the gingerbread man somewhere in the school and hint where the children might look for him. The hint could be: "The gingerbread man has run a long way down a long hall and now can smell something delicious." At lunch time, students will undoubtedly spot the gingerbread man on the counter of the cafeteria. At the end of the day, review where the gingerbread man appeared and the names of the staff and their function in that area of the school.

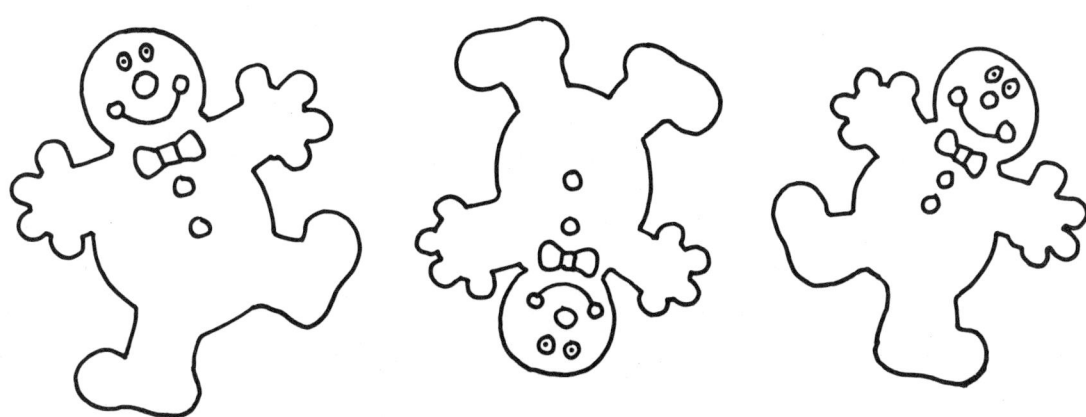

WHAT'S MY LINE?

Use this game to help students learn the names and responsibilities of school staff members.

MATERIALS:
Small sheets of paper, pencil

DIRECTIONS:
Write the name of a faculty member or school staff member on each sheet of paper. Under the name write the grade level or job. Some examples are:

   Mrs. Clark   Mr. Jacobs   Miss Simms
   Principal   Custodian   Second Grade

Pick a student to be the mystery guest. Have that student choose a slip (without looking) and, pretending to be that person, answer yes or no questions from the class. Students take turns asking one question at a time. For example, they might ask, "Do you work on the second floor?" "Are you busiest at lunch time?" "Are you in the room next door?" A student who gets a yes answer may ask a second question or pass to the next person. If no is the response, the turn is passed. When ready, students guess who the mystery guest is. However, if a guess is wrong, the student is out of the game. Questioning continues until someone guesses correctly, and that person becomes the next mystery guest.

BIG LOONY BIRD

This bird will acquaint students with the rules of their classroom and school.

MATERIALS:
Cardboard, colored paper, yarn, ribbon, feathers, scissors, glue, string (optional)

DIRECTIONS:
Make a big funny bird out of the odds and ends. The bird, named Priscilla, may be made into a puppet by attaching strings to the wings and tail feathers. On the first day of school, have Priscilla explain the class and school rules to the students, as well as rules about safety and manners. As a follow-up activity, the students may make stick puppets of Priscilla's head.

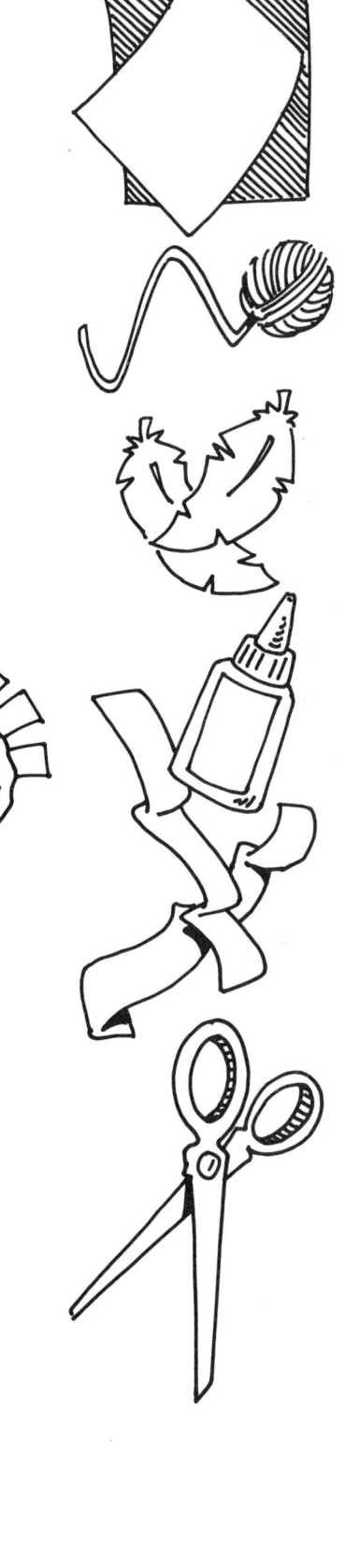

LIBRARY BOOK MAZE

This display will remind students when they checked out library books and when they should return them.

MATERIALS:
Construction paper, perforated edges of computer paper, kraft paper, copies of the house and school patterns, marker, scissors, stapler, oaktag

DIRECTIONS:
Use the perforated edges to design a maze in the middle of a bulletin board. Copy the house and school patterns onto construction paper and cut them out. Mount the house at the beginning of the maze and the school at the end. Letter the following phrases on kraft paper:
   LET'S HELP LIBRARY BOOKS GET THROUGH THE MAZE
   CHECK OUT:
   RETURN:
Cut out and mount the title above the maze and place "Check Out" and "Return" to the side. Print the names of the two days on oaktag cards and staple them in the proper position.

ALL-STAR PRODUCTION

This display will introduce the school staff and the students.

MATERIALS:
Gold, silver, and white paper, copy of the star pattern, scissors, pencil, marker, stapler

DIRECTIONS:
From gold paper, cut out the following title: ALL-STAR PRODUCTION. From silver paper, cut out the following words:
- STARRING:
- DIRECTED BY:
- PRODUCED BY:
- RESEARCH BY:

Make a copy of the star pattern and cut it out. Use the star to outline 30 to 40 stars on silver paper and cut them out. Print the name of one of the following people on each of the stars:

students	principal
teacher	librarian

Mount the gold title along the top of the bulletin board. Down the middle of the board, mount the silver captions. Beside each, staple the corresponding name(s). Cut additional stars from silver, gold, and white to form a border around the display.

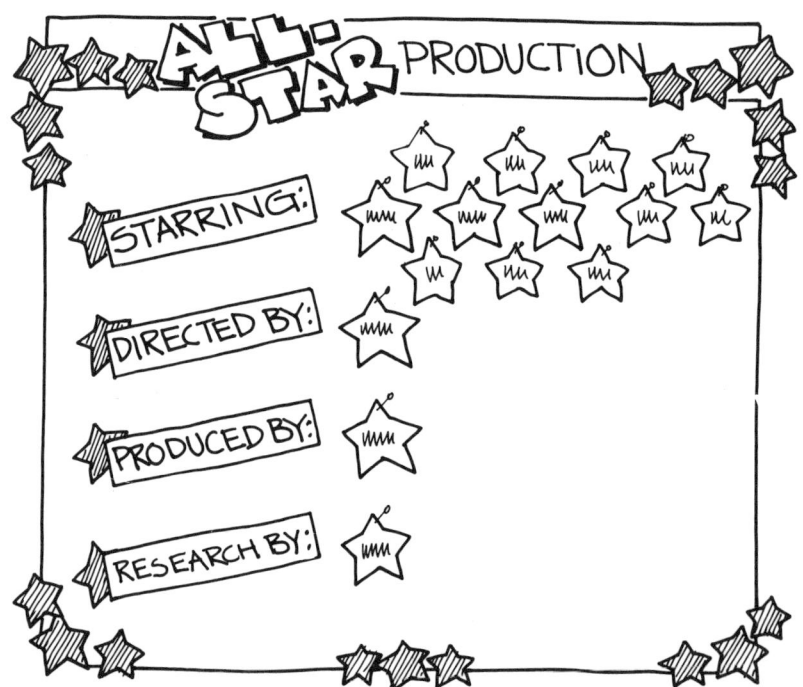

OUR CLASSROOM RULES

Use this bulletin board display to introduce classroom rules.

MATERIALS:
Red, yellow, and white construction paper, kraft paper, three dowel sticks, scissors, black marker, pushpins, stapler

DIRECTIONS:
From the construction paper, cut a large red hexagon, a large yellow triangle, and a large white rectangle. Outline the edges of each shape with the black marker. On kraft paper, letter and cut out the following title: THE RULES ARE IMPORTANT, AND WE HAVE A FEW, HERE ARE THREE THAT WE MUST DO. . . Choose three rules that you want the students to learn and print one on each sign. Some examples are: "Be kind to others," "Put all finished work in the basket," and "Use a soft voice." Staple the title along the top of the bulletin board and the three signs across the middle. Attach a dowel under each sign with pins.

VARIATION:
Use this display to teach about road signs by adding some additional road signs and rules.

BUS RIDERS' CHART

Display pictures of school buses to remind students of their bus number.

MATERIALS:
Yellow poster board, oaktag, black construction paper, copy of the bus pattern, scissors, glue, marker

DIRECTIONS:
Enlarge the bus pattern and outline on the yellow poster board as many buses as serve your class. Cut children's heads from oaktag and glue them in the bus windows. Find out the children's bus numbers and print them on the buses. On black construction paper, letter and cut out the title BUS RIDERS' CHART. Mount the display on a wall or bulletin board near the classroom entrance. Copy the bus pattern on a ditto master and print above it: I KNOW MY BUS NUMBER. Distribute copies to the students and allow them to draw children in the windows. Before the children take their sheets home, check to be sure that each child has written in his or her correct bus number.

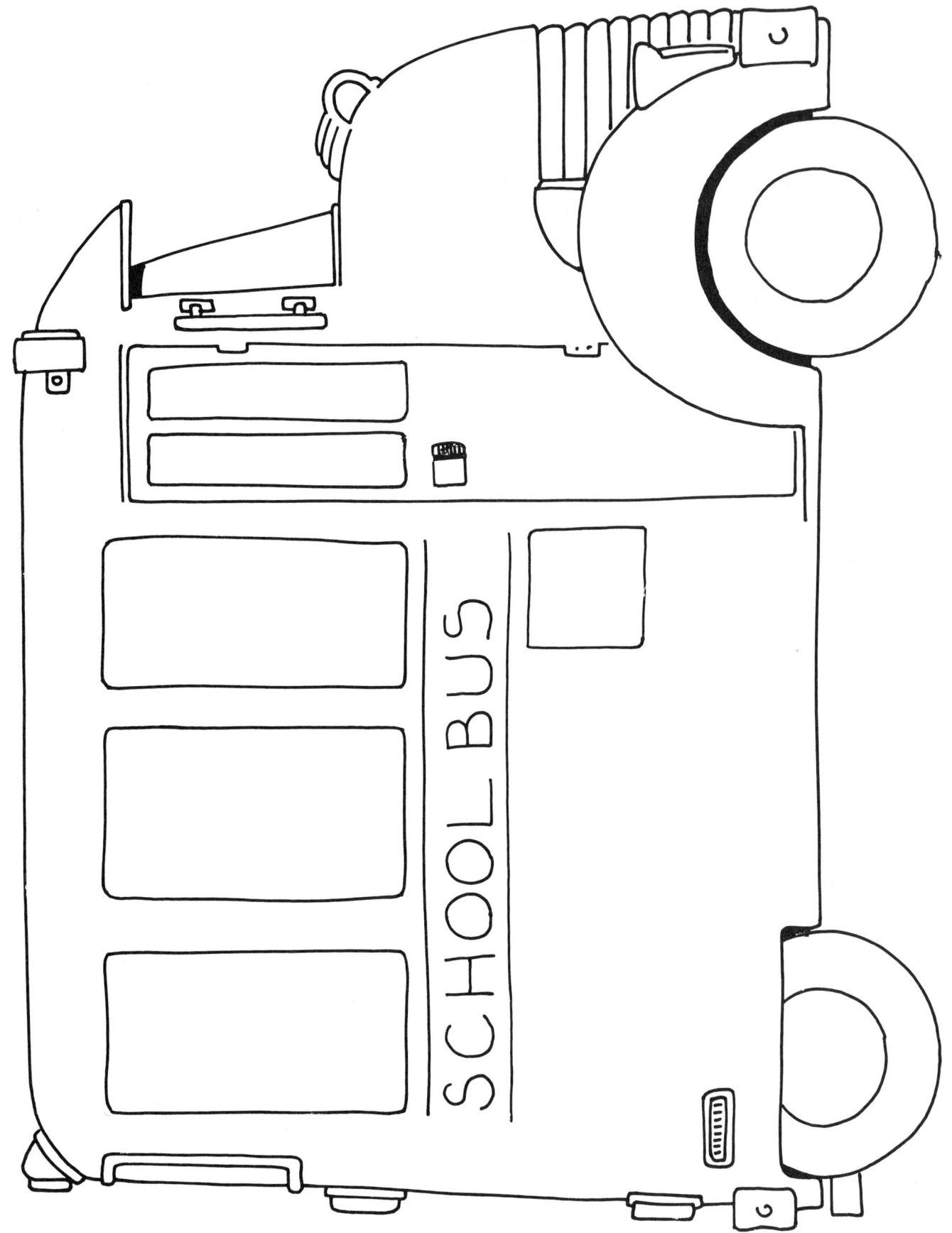

WHAT'S COOKIN'?

Use this display to show the school lunch menu.

MATERIALS:
White kraft paper, red and various other colors of construction paper, stapler, markers, school lunch menu, magazines, scissors, glue, resource list of food calories and nutrients

DIRECTIONS:
Cut a large chef's hat from the white kraft paper and staple it to the bulletin board. From the red construction paper, cut the following title: WHAT'S COOKIN'? Staple the title across the top of the display. Divide the children into four food group teams: breads and cereals, meats and main dishes, dairy products, fruits and vegetables. Have each team cut out magazine pictures of foods that typically appear on the school lunch menu. You might invite the school cafeteria manager to come into the classroom and offer suggestions to the groups.

Have the children mount the food pictures on construction paper, using a different color for each team. Provide teams with the resource list of food calories and nutrients. (Check with the cafeteria manager or your school library for this information.) Have the teams use the information to cut out a label for each food and glue it below the food picture. Mount each daily menu on the chef's hat. Each day appoint a student to display the food pictures of the menu items. Use the calorie and nutrient information as the basis for classroom activities. For example, you might have students find out how many calories are in the day's lunch, which food on a menu offers the most vitamin C, or what lower-calorie food they would substitute for a dessert.

CHECK IT OFF

This board display will help students remember what supplies they need to bring to school.

MATERIALS:
Red kraft paper, oaktag, crayon box, pencils, scissors, glue box, paper, marker, pushpins, lengths of yarn, stapler

DIRECTIONS:
Staple the yarn to form a large graph with six vertical columns and enough spaces to list the students in the class. Print each child's name on a piece of oaktag cut to fit the space you allowed. Staple the names in place. On red kraft paper, letter and cut out the title CHECK IT OFF. Staple the title above the yarn graph. Attach the crayon box, pencils, scissors, glue box, and paper in the spaces across the top with pins. (Change the supplies, if necessary, to reflect those required by your school or district.) Print on oaktag the heading NAME. Staple the heading at the top of the name column. Put a check beside each student's name as he or she brings in the materials.

CHECK IT OFF!

NAME	Crayons	Pencils	Scissors	Glue	Paper
Lisa	✓	✓		✓	✓
Mike		✓	✓		
Jason	✓				
Ryan	✓	✓	✓	✓	✓
Becky	✓		✓	✓	✓
Tara	✓	✓	✓		✓
Cathy	✓		✓	✓	✓
Heidi	✓				✓
Cal	✓	✓	✓		
Joe		✓		✓	
Sid		✓	✓		✓
Pat	✓		✓		✓

CHAPTER 2
New Classmates

THE FRIENDSHIP CIRCLE

Students get acquainted and practice questioning skills as they play a ball game.

MATERIALS:
Soccer ball or kickball, chart paper, marker

DIRECTIONS:
Have the students brainstorm a list of questions they would like to ask each other. For example:
  When is your birthday?
  What is your middle name?
  How many brothers and sisters do you have?
  Where were you born?
  What do you want to be when you grow up?
  What is your favorite place to visit?
  What is your favorite food?
  What color do you like best?

Write the questions on the chart paper to serve as memory joggers during the game. Direct the students to sit in a circle on the floor. Model the game for the students. First, tell a fact about yourself. Then, ask a student for the same information as you roll the ball to him or her. The student must answer your question, give another fact about himself or herself, then ask another student for the same information while rolling the ball on. For example:

Teacher: "I have two brothers and a sister. Jonathan, how many brothers and sisters do you have?"

Jonathan: "I have one sister. My favorite food is tacos. Carrie, what is your favorite food?"

Carrie: "My favorite food is spaghetti. I have a dog named Jojo. Theresa, what pets do you have?"

VARIATION:
Use a simpler version for primary students. Have them sit in a circle and take turns rolling the ball to another student. The first time the ball is received, the student tells his or her name. When the ball comes a second time, the student might tell about a hobby, favorite sports team, or favorite food.

BIG INITIALS

Students make collages that describe themselves.

MATERIALS:
Construction paper, scissors, glue, magazines, newspapers

DIRECTIONS:
Have the students cut out their initials from large sheets of construction paper. Then have them look in the magazines and newspapers for pictures and words that describe their hobbies, likes, family, talents, favorite school subjects, foods, and travel spots. Ask the students to glue these items on their initials in collage form. Have the students hang their completed initials around the room or along the hallway near the classroom.

CINDERELLA

This ice-breaker helps introduce students.

DIRECTIONS:
Direct the students to take off both shoes. Have them each place one shoe in their desk and bring the second shoe to pile with the others on the floor. Have students sit on the floor in a circle around the shoe pile. Pick up a shoe, briefly describe it, and then make a guess as to which student the shoe belongs. Make a second guess, if necessary. If you haven't guessed correctly after two tries, ask students who think they know to make guesses, one at a time. When finally identified, the shoe's owner receives the shoe back. Then he or she is the next one to pick up a shoe, describe it, and try to identify the owner. Continue the game until all the shoes have been identified and claimed.

MEET YOUR MATCH

This activity helps students discover things they have in common.

MATERIALS:
Construction paper, scissors

DIRECTIONS:
Cut pairs of shapes and randomly distribute one shape to each student. Ask the students to find their match and spend a few minutes talking with that person. During this conversation, have the pairs of students try to identify two other ways in which they match each other. Then have the pairs tell the rest of the class how they match. Some examples of things in common might be "We both have brown eyes and two sisters" or "We both like math and playing soccer."

INTERVIEW THE CELEBRITIES

In this activity, classmates gain a new perspective on each other.

MATERIALS:
Paper, pencils

DIRECTIONS:
Pair the children and ask them to spend several minutes interviewing each other as though the other child were a celebrity. Questions might include:
"What are you famous for?"
"What special talents helped you get where you are today?"
"What accomplishment are you especially proud of?"
"What advice do you have for other students?"
After the interviews are completed, have each student introduce his or her partner to the rest of the class, using the information gained from the interview. At the end of the introduction, other classmates may ask questions in press-conference style, for example:
"What do you plan to work on next?"
"Do you enjoy being famous?"

SCAVENGER HUNT

Students use observation and questioning skills in this game.

MATERIALS:
A copy of the Scavenger Hunt List for each student, pencils

DIRECTIONS:
Pass out a list to each student. Allow 15 to 30 minutes for students to find a different classmate to sign each line on the sheet. Students may only sign on a line that applies to them. Each student may sign his or her name just once per sheet, and only one name may be put on each line.

LONG HAIR   WIDE BELT   LUNCH BOX

SCAVENGER HUNT LIST

Look around the room and find:

1. The tallest person in our class. _____
2. The person with the most freckles. _____
3. The person with the widest belt. _____
4. The one with the longest hair. _____
5. The oldest person. _____
6. The youngest person. _____
7. Someone who has blue eyes. _____
8. Someone who has brown eyes. _____
9. Someone who has brown hair. _____
10. Someone who has on blue tennis shoes. _____
11. Any girl wearing a dress. _____
12. A person who brought lunch from home. _____
13. A person who lives on your street. _____
14. Someone who is wearing red. _____
15. Someone who rides the bus. _____
16. Someone with a birthday in September. _____
17. Someone with the same middle initial as yours. _____
18. Someone who loves pizza. _____
19. Someone who read the same book you read this summer. _____
20. Someone who was born in another state. _____
21. Someone who didn't go to this school last year. _____
22. Someone who went to a baseball game this summer. _____
23. Someone who went camping this summer. _____
24. A person who has more than four pockets. _____
25. The person with the smallest shoe size. _____

GETTING TO KNOW YOU

Students practice interviewing skills in this activity.

MATERIALS:
Construction paper, scissors, box, list of get-acquainted questions for each student (see the examples below), pencils

DIRECTIONS:
Cut pairs of construction paper strips in 10 to 15 different colors (depending on the number of students). Place the strips in a box and have each student draw out one. Then have students find the person with the same color strip. After they have found their partners, pass out the list of get-acquainted questions to each student. Model for the students how to interview and get interesting responses to the questions. Allow students 15 minutes to interview each other, writing the answers down as they go. When the time is up, have each student introduce his or her partner to the class. An appointed clerk can write each name on the board as the person is introduced.

A few example questions are:
- Who is in your family?
- What are your hobbies?
- What is your favorite book?
- What job does your mother/father have?
- What job would you like to have as an adult?
- Which holiday is your favorite and why?
- If you had one million dollars, what would you do with it?

VARIATION:
Have students generate interview sheets with five questions of their own.

CIRCLE NAME GAME

Students learn the names of their classmates in this game.

DIRECTIONS:
Sit in a circle with the students. Beginning with the student on your left, have students tell their first names and a favorite food that begins with the same letter. After each student tells his own name and food, he repeats all those that came before. The goal is to go all the way around the circle, repeating each name and food. Take the last turn if you wish. The students will enjoy seeing if their teacher can name all the students and their favorite foods.

PHOTO MAGIC

Use instant photographs of students to create interest throughout the year.

MATERIALS:
Polaroid camera, film, boxes, markers, glue

DIRECTIONS:
Set up a small, temporary "photo studio" in the classroom. A chair in front of a plain wall or curtained booth will do. On the first day of school, take each child's photograph. Then mount the photos on student mailboxes and label the boxes with the children's names. This will help children associate the written name with the face.

Later, you can use the photos to make an attendance board. Punch a hole at the top of each photo and attach a paper clip hanger. Hook the hanger on a pin on the board. As students come in each morning, they should turn over their photos to show their presence. As they leave each evening, they turn the photos to the blank side. In May, you can tie a ribbon through the hole at the top and send each photo home for Mother's Day. On the last day of school, you can make a photo display that will welcome your new class the next year. Take each child's photo again. Have the children make cartoon captions that give humorous or serious messages to next year's students. Mount the photos and captions on a board at the beginning of the next year.

WELCOME TO THE BUNCH

Welcome the class with this door display.

MATERIALS:
Oaktag, markers, black construction paper, copy of monkey pattern, yellow poster board, scissors, push-pins

DIRECTIONS:
Enlarge the monkey pattern and draw it on the oaktag. Color the monkey and cut it out. Draw a large bunch of bananas on the yellow poster board and cut it out. On each banana, write the name of a student who is assigned to the classroom. Letter and cut out the title WELCOME TO THE BUNCH. Mount the display on the classroom door. To carry the theme further, make name tags for the students in the shape of a banana.

WELCOME TO THE SCHOOL

This door display is perfect for a door with a window in it.

MATERIALS:
Tissue paper, construction paper, copy of fish pattern, scissors, markers, thread, pushpins

DIRECTIONS:
From tissue paper, cut out a fish for each student in the class. Print one student's name on each fish. Cut a large fish from tissue paper and print the teacher's name on it. Cut out the letters of the title WELCOME TO THE SCHOOL. Hang the fish in the window of the door with thread. Mount the title above the window. Cut a fish name tag from construction paper for each student.

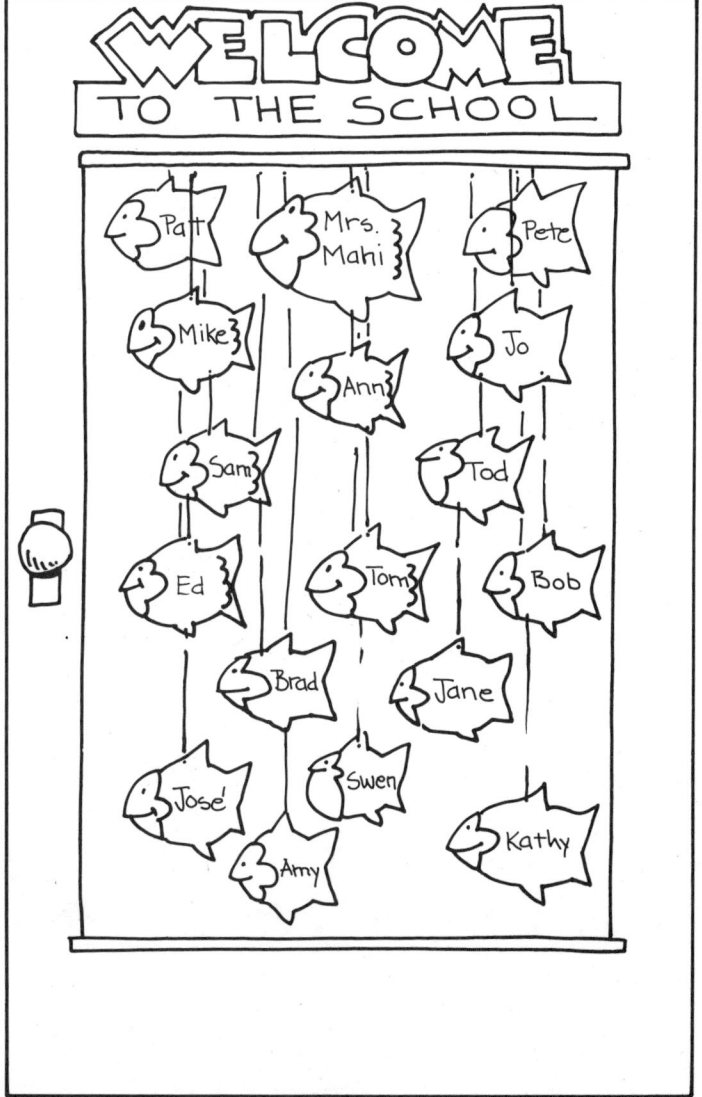

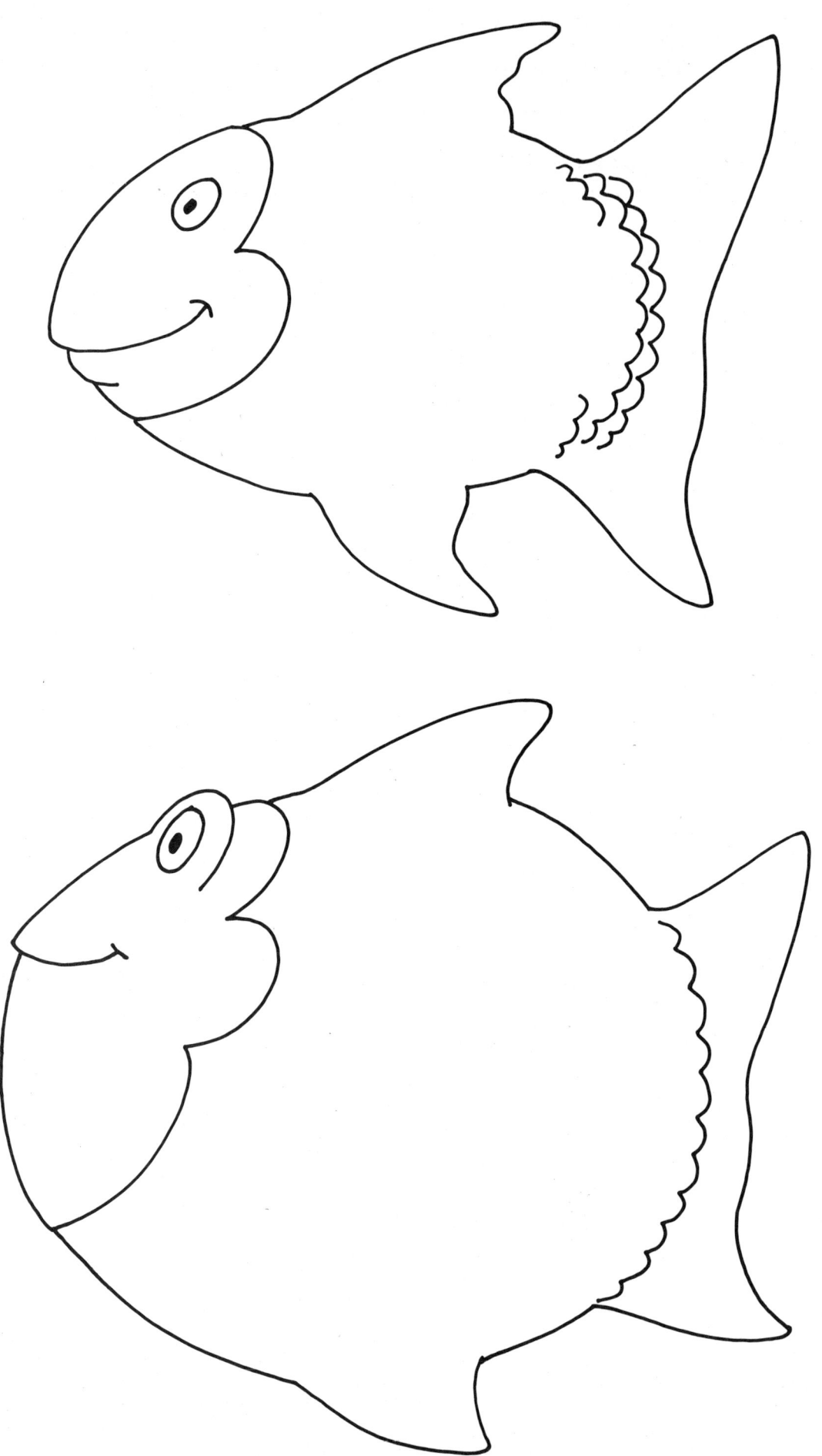

CHAPTER 3
Teamwork and Self-Esteem

PARTNER PORTRAITS

Here is an activity in which students draw pictures of each other.

MATERIALS:
Drawing paper, pencils or crayons

DIRECTIONS:
Print a student's name in one corner of each sheet of drawing paper. Pair the students and distribute the paper so that pairs have each other's name. Direct the pairs to sit opposite each other and draw one another's portraits. When the portraits are completed, the students exchange drawings to receive their own. Partner Portraits can then make an effective bulletin board display.

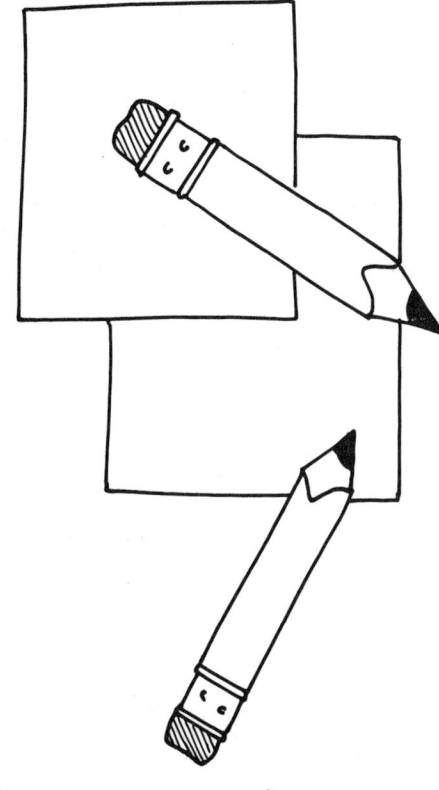

LOOK WHO'S HERE TODAY!

Students create a shape picture that shows class attendance.

MATERIALS:
Construction paper, pushpins, scissors, markers

DIRECTIONS:
Divide a bulletin board in half. On one side, cut out and mount letters that say LOOK WHO'S HERE TODAY! Then cut a variety of shapes and pin them on the blank side of the board. On the first day, have each student choose a shape and write his or her name on it. As the students come in on each subsequent day, have them place their shapes on the LOOK WHO'S HERE TODAY! side. They may arrange the shapes to create a new design each day. At the end of the month, allow students to choose new shapes.

IT'S MY BAG

This activity encourages in-depth understanding of classmates as individuals.

MATERIALS:
Bags provided by students

DIRECTIONS:
Ask students to bring to school a bag containing six objects that tell something about themselves. Forewarn students that they will be sharing these items with classmates. After the bags have been brought in, sit in a circle on the floor. Take turns opening the bags and showing the items one by one, explaining the meaning of each. For example, someone might say, "I brought a bag of seeds because I like to plant gardens and see things grow. This picture of the mountains represents my interest in camping and the out-of-doors. I brought a cassette of Michael Jackson because I love music and dancing. I brought a cookie because I have a sweet tooth and love to bake things like cookies. I brought this airline ticket because I'd like to be a pilot for a big airline when I grow up. I brought this tennis ball because my favorite sport is tennis." You can start off the session by modeling the procedure with your own bag.

HOW DO YOU FIT IN?

Use this activity to welcome your new students.

MATERIALS:
Blank puzzle or copy of the puzzle pattern, markers, paper, envelopes, scissors

DIRECTIONS:
Buy a blank puzzle or use the puzzle pattern mounted on cardboard to make a blank puzzle with enough pieces for each student to have one. Using permanent markers, decorate the puzzle with a welcoming message, such as:

    Mrs. Harper's Brand New Group
    We All Fit Together in Mr. Branson's Class

During the summer, write a letter about your classroom to be duplicated and mailed to each student. You might include information about supplies, field trips, lunch money, special classes, and units of study. At the end of the letter, include these sentences: "I've enclosed a puzzle piece in this letter. Your first assignment is to bring the puzzle piece the first day of school. When we're all together, you will see how the puzzle fits together." Break the puzzle into pieces and put one piece into each child's letter. On the first day of school, have students bring their puzzle pieces to a table. Allow the students to put the pieces together to find the message you have written.

NAME TAG JIGSAW PUZZLE

Children assemble a puzzle to discover a message.

MATERIALS:
Large sheet each of red and yellow construction paper, markers, puzzle pattern, scissors

DIRECTIONS:
On one side of each sheet of construction paper, write a secret welcoming message, for example, WELCOME TO ROOM 18. I'M GLAD YOU'RE HERE! Cut the sheet of red paper into a jigsaw puzzle with as many pieces as there are girls in the class. On the blank side of each piece, write the name of one of the girls. Cut the yellow paper into a puzzle with as many pieces as there are boys. Write a boy's name on the blank side of each piece. Distribute the name tags and have the children wear them during the first week of school. At the end of the week, explain that there is a secret message for the children on the back of their name tags. Provide a table where the children can put the puzzle pieces together and discover the message.

KIDS ON DISPLAY

Children design folders that show off their work.

MATERIALS:
One file folder per student, magazines and catalogs, scissors, glue, paper, pushpins, pencils

DIRECTIONS:
Tell the students to cut out magazine and catalog pictures that reflect their own personalities and interests. Then have the students glue the pictures on one inside file folder panel. On the other inside panel, have the students glue a brief written explanation of the collage. Display the completed personality folders (with the names hidden) on a bulletin board under the title GUESS WHO. Provide small pieces of paper and pins so that students can write down a name and pin it by the folder they think it matches. When the identification game is over, use the folders to store work for grading or conferences.

MY OWN NUMBER CHART

Children make charts of important numbers in their lives.

MATERIALS:
Two construction paper circles (11" and 4" diameters) per student, rulers, markers, old calendars, scissors, glue

DIRECTIONS:
Have the students use markers and rulers to divide the large circle into eight sections. Have them label the sections with personal-information titles that involve numbers, such as Phone Number, Address, Age, Height, and so on. Then have them glue the small circle in the center of the large circle and write on it MY OWN NUMBER CHART. Have the students cut from an old calendar the numerals they need to complete their charts, then glue them into place. They may draw pictures to illustrate the categories on the charts.

PHOTO POEMS

Create a special board with children's photographs and name poems.

MATERIALS:
Polaroid camera and film, construction paper, rubber cement, markers

DIRECTIONS:
Take a Polaroid photograph of each child. Mount each photo on a sheet of construction paper and write the child's name vertically beside the picture. Have the children complete the name poems, using words that describe themselves and begin with the letters of their names. For example:

S - strong	C - cartoons
A - artistic	A - astronaut
R - riddles	R - right-handed
A - anytime	L - laughing
H - hurry	O - okay
	S - surprise

Display the mounted photos and poems on a bulletin board.

OUR STAR THIS WEEK

This board gives students the opportunity to share information about themselves.

MATERIALS:
Kraft paper, scissors, oaktag cards, marker

DIRECTIONS:
Cut the letters for the board title: OUR STAR THIS WEEK. Mount the title at the top of the board. On each card write a category: family, pets, hobbies, sports, foods, talents, travel. Mount the cards on the board, allowing space to display items in each category. Arrange for a different student to fill the board each week. On Monday morning, the student of the week brings in a variety of items that represent him or her. (Examples: recipes of favorite foods, family and pet photos, baseball cards, post cards, magazine pictures, drawings.) The student mounts the items on the board. Throughout the week, encourage other students to add items to the board. These might be positive reactions, such as notes or poems, or just things the student might like, such as a drawing or cartoon.

PART II
Moving Along

CHAPTER 4
Sponge (In-Between-Times) Activities

BRAINY LINEUPS

Try these new ways to have your class line up.

DIRECTIONS:
To call on a row to line up, use a math problem: "All students in the row that has $3 \times 2 - 1$ students in it, please line up." Or use comparison clues: "The row that has the most girls," or "The row with an equal number of boys and girls." Or use location clues: "The row that is the farthest from the door," "The row that is nearest to the teacher's desk." Or use language clues: "The row that is the same as quintuplets," "The row that is the same as quadruplets." To have students line up in small groups, use other criteria: "All students line up whose last names begin with A-H," "Whose first names begin with S-Z," "Who have a kind of pet beginning with A-K." You can use brainy lineups every day to reinforce lesson content. They're fun, they stimulate critical thinking, and they build skills in sequencing, comparing, and evaluating.

ALPHABET SENSE

Students practice both spelling and math skills.

MATERIALS:
Twenty-six oaktag cards, marker, tape

DIRECTIONS:
On each oaktag card, mark a money value between 1 and 50. Vary the form of the values on the cards, for example, $.02, 5¢. Tape a card beneath each letter of the alphabet chart in the room. When you have a few minutes between activities, print a word on the board and ask the children to use the chart to figure out how much the word is worth. Here are more ideas:

Find two words that are worth the same amount.
If the word "bat" is worth 28¢, would a word that rhymes with bat be worth more or less?
How much money is your name worth?
Who has the most expensive name in the class? The least expensive?
If you could change your name, what would it be and how much would it be worth?
What state in the United States is worth the most money?

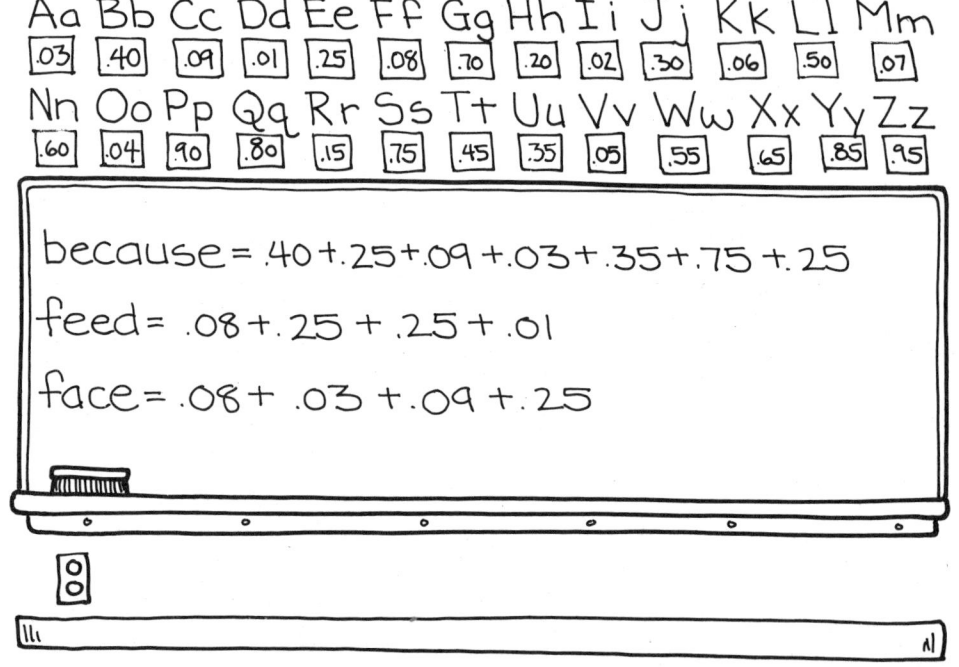

CALENDAR CAPERS

Students use the classroom calendar to practice thinking skills.

MATERIALS:
Large classroom calendar

DIRECTIONS:
Use spare classroom moments to ask students questions about the calendar month. Here are some examples:

How many Mondays will we have this month?
How many full weeks will there be in this month?
How many more days until Jerry's birthday?
If an election is held on the first Tuesday after the first Monday in the month, when would an election be held this month?
What day of the week will we have the fewest of this month?
What day of the week will we have the most of this month?

NOVEMBER HAS:
5 TUESDAYS
5 WEDNESDAYS
4 SATURDAYS
SUNDAYS
MONDAYS
THURS.
FRIDAYS

NOVEMBER HAS:
3 FULL WEEKS
2 HOLIDAYS

NOVEMBER 1988

SUN	MON	TUES	WED	THUR	FRI	SAT
		1	2	3	4	5 Tom's B.D.
6	7	8 Election Day	9	10	11 Veterans Day	12
13	14	15	16	17	18	19
20	21	22	23	24 Thanksgiving	25	26
27	28	29 Sarah's B.D.	30			

FIND YOUR PARTNER

Make up cards that introduce famous people or focus on a particular subject area.

MATERIALS:
Sheets of paper or index cards, marker, scissors

DIRECTIONS:
Make up name, phrase, or fact combinations related to the lesson and write one on each card or sheet of paper. Cut each card in half to resemble puzzle pieces. Pass out one piece to each student. Direct the students to walk around and find the person with the matching half. Follow the activity with a task requiring students to work in pairs.

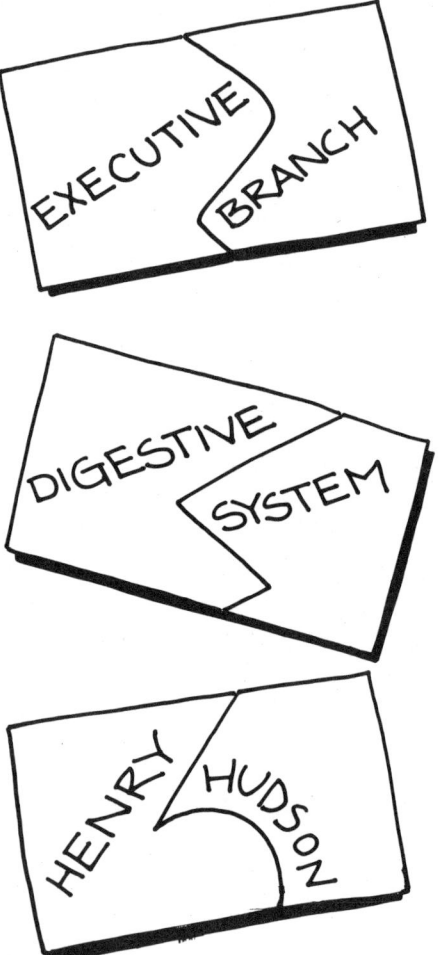

RIDDLE BUCKET

Fill odd moments with this riddle-guessing game.

MATERIALS:
Plastic bucket, pieces of 6" x 5" construction paper, pen or pencil, marker, clear contact paper

DIRECTIONS:
Decorate a plastic bucket with question marks. Then ask a class of older students to submit riddles for your bucket. Fold the sheets of construction paper to form 3" x 5" cards. Print each riddle on the outside of a card and the answer on the inside. Laminate or cover the cards with clear contact paper. Place the riddles in the bucket and, when you have a few minutes, pull a card from the bucket and ask the class the riddle. Call on students to try to guess the answer. Allow the child who thinks of the answer to take the next riddle out of the bucket. When everyone has the idea, the students may be able to play the game independently. Have one student get the bucket and ask the class the riddle.

VARIATION:
Follow the same procedure using social studies, math, or science review questions.

WORD FUN

Pundles

In these activities, children try to decipher letter riddles, and practice spelling words.

MATERIALS:
Transparencies, markers, overhead projector

DIRECTIONS:
Copy the pundles examples on a transparency and use an overhead projector to show one. Ask the children to think of what word the pundle represents. Allow time for the children to try to figure it out. Share answers, and then try some more. Finally, have the children invent their own, working together if they like. Duplicate their pundles onto transparencies and print the names of the students who cooperated in making the riddle. Have the rest of the class try to guess the meaning.

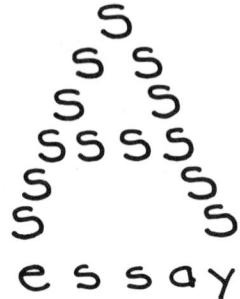

Droodles

MATERIALS:
Transparencies, markers, overhead projector

DIRECTIONS:
Reproduce some of the sample droodles on transparencies. Use the overhead projector to show the examples to the class. Have the children pick a difficult word from their spelling or vocabulary list and turn the word into a droodle that will help them remember.

HINK-PINKS

Rhyming words are the basis for this game.

DIRECTIONS:
A hink-pink is a pair of one-syllable rhyming words with a made-up definition. For example, a "hag bag" could be a witch's purse, and a "sad dad" is an unhappy father. Introduce the students to some examples of hink-pinks. Then call on one child to think of and say a rhyming pair. Ask the other students to think of a meaning. After students understand the game, they can lead their own game when you are called away for a few minutes.

VARIATIONS:
Play the game with hinky-pinkies—two-syllable rhyming pairs—or hinkety-pinketies (very difficult!)—three-syllable rhyming pairs.

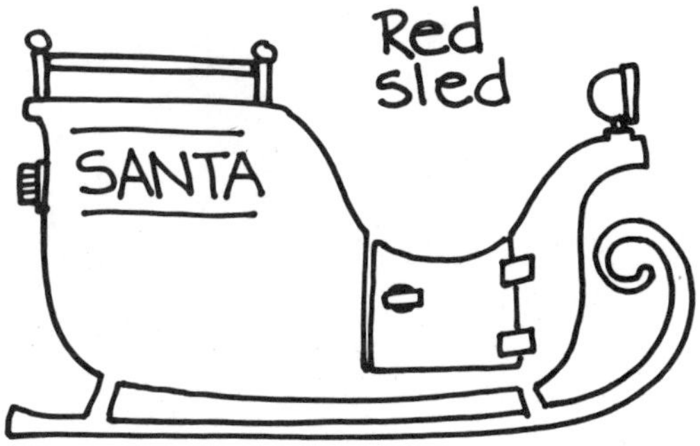

SILENT MATH PRACTICE

Children use hand signals to practice math problems.

DIRECTIONS:
Teach the children hand signals for all the math operations: add, subtract, equals, multiply, divide. Then use your hands to present math problems with numbers under ten by using your fingers for the numbers and the signals for the operations. Have the children signal their answers by using their fingers. When you have demonstrated how to do the activity, choose a student to lead the practice.

SIGN PUNCTUATION

Students use sign language to punctuate sentences.

DIRECTIONS:
For each kind of sentence, teach the students a different sign:
- Question - Students raise their eyebrows and draw a question mark in the air with their fingers.
- Exclamation - Students suck in their breath and draw an exclamation point in the air.
- Statement - Students make a click with their tongues and draw a dot in the air.

After the students know the signs, say a sentence and have the students show the appropriate punctuation for it. For example:
- What time is it?
- You saw a deer!
- I want to swing next.

GUESS THE NUMBER

This game helps children develop questioning skills.

DIRECTIONS:
Think of a number between 1 and 50. Tell one child the number. Then have the other students take turns asking the child yes or no questions to find out what the number is. Encourage students to think of questions that will give them information about the number, rather than questions that just eliminate one number. Instead of asking if it's the number after 14, for example, students might ask if it is a two-digit number, or whether it's larger than 10, or if it has a 5 in it. A student who thinks he or she knows the number may make a guess, but if the guess is incorrect, the guessing continues. The student who guesses correctly gets to make up the next number and answer questions about it.

CHAPTER 5
Games for Review

LET'S LOOK AT THE FACTS

Make this display to assist students with social studies review.

MATERIALS:
3" x 5" index cards, markers, library pocket, construction paper, scissors, pushpins

DIRECTIONS:
Write the following words on index cards: Who, What, When, Where, Why. Mount the cards across the top of a bulletin board. Place blank index cards in a library pocket mounted on the board. Cut a title, for example, LET'S REVIEW EXPLORERS, from construction paper and mount it on the board. Ask students to think of words related to the topic, and write them on the index cards to pin under the appropriate heading. Students may use the board to review information, to write reports, or to demonstrate their understanding of a topic.

VARIATIONS:
Duplicate the words on a five-box grid on paper. To assist in reviewing a topic, organize the class into teams and have each team think of as many words for the boxes as possible.

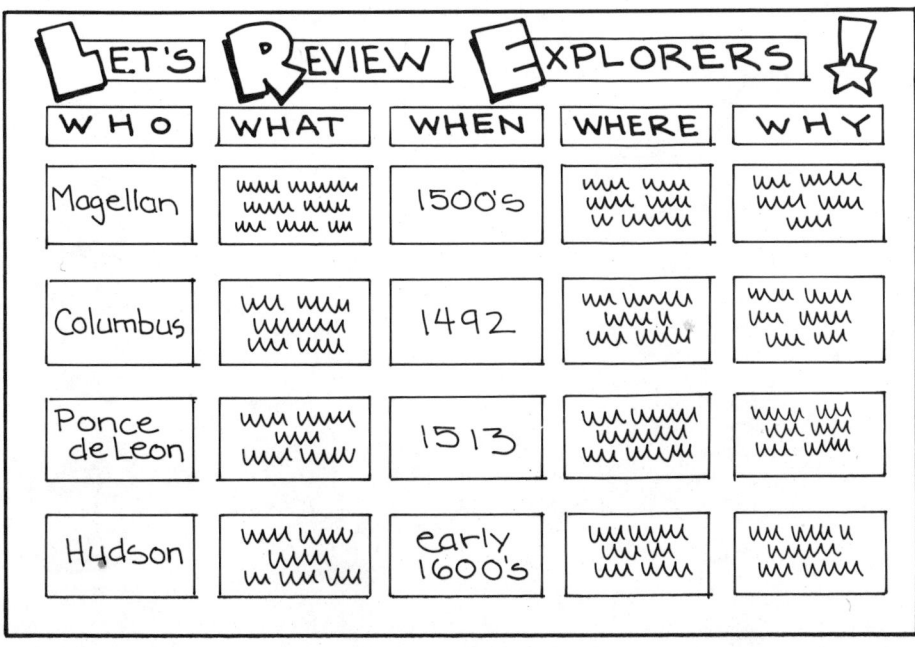

LET'S TRADE QUESTIONS

Use this small-group activity for science or social studies review.

MATERIALS:
Textbooks, resource books, paper, pencils

DIRECTIONS:
Choose a topic and divide the students into groups. Allow each group 15 minutes to look through their information, resource books, and/or texts and write as many questions as they have time for on the topic. Group members should be able to answer all of their own questions. When the time is up, have the groups exchange questions. Then have each group work for another 15 minutes finding and writing the answers to the other group's questions. At the end of the time, students should return the questions to the original group and have the answers checked. Review the questions as a whole group and discuss any questions that were hard to answer, or cover areas where the students had difficulty.

YOU ARE THE TEACHER

Children plan a lesson in order to review information.

MATERIALS:
Lesson plan forms, pencils

DIRECTIONS:
To review any unit or subject, invite the children to think how they would teach the information. Have each child write up a lesson plan using the following form:

  To introduce the lesson, I will:
  To share the new information, I will:
  To see if my students are learning the information, I will:
  To see if the students can work on their own with the new information, I will:

When the lesson plans are completed, allow the students to choose a partner and practice teaching their lessons. Encourage the students to make any revisions necessary. After their revisions have been made, allow any student who wishes to teach his or her lesson to a small group of students.

TEAM SUCCESS

This team approach helps ensure that each child masters information.

MATERIALS:
Poster board, markers

DIRECTIONS:
Divide the students into study teams of four to six children. Explain that each team's goal is to help all its members understand a topic or subject. Set a time period of a week and review what will be expected of each team during the week. For example, the students will study together and learn a list of vocabulary words that will be tested on Friday. Explain that each team will receive a team grade on all material covered during the week. Allow each team to pick a name and make a poster to be displayed during their study time. Give a pre-test of the information and then review it. Encourage the teams to schedule their study time and keep track of the hours spent working together. Also encourage students to share study tips with other team members.

At the end of the week, give the post-test and provide each team with a team (not individual) grade. Choose another topic or subject the following week for the teams to work on and follow the same procedure. Allow students to chart their success by making a visual record of their team grades. Change teams about every six weeks.

SPIN IT

Use this game to review math material.

MATERIALS:
Chalkboard, chalk

DIRECTIONS:
Write eight math problems on the chalkboard above the heads of the students in your class. Choose eight students to stand under the eight problems. Then have the children in their seats take turns calling out the answer to a problem, but not indicate which problem they are answering. Each child at the board should check to see if the answer belongs to his or her problem. If it does, the child should spin around once. If the child is correct, he or she stays in position at the board. If the child is not correct, the one who called out the answer takes that place at the board. Continue play by adding new problems to the board as answers are given.

VARIATION:
Use this game to review information in a social studies or science unit. Put the names of eight planets on the board, for example, and have audience members give a fact about one of the planets.

DUELING MATH REVIEW

Children review basic math facts as they play this game.

DIRECTIONS:
Divide the class into two teams. Have one child from each team come to the open area between the teams and stand up back to back. Then say a math fact slowly. As soon as you say the first number in the problem, the students should begin to pace away from each other. When the problem is completed, the first student to turn and give the correct answer wins and stays up to meet the next child from the opposite team in another duel.

FRACTION PIZZA

Children review fractions as they divide a pizza.

MATERIALS:
Oaktag or cardboard circles (7" or 8" diameter), yellow construction paper, various scraps of colored construction paper, scissors, glue, black markers, rulers

DIRECTIONS:
Give each student a circle and tell everyone that they are going to make their favorite pizza. First, have them cut out and glue on a piece of yellow construction paper to fit the circle. Then have them cut toppings (pepperoni, mushrooms, olives, green pepper, sausage) from construction paper scraps and glue them on. When the pizzas are completed, have each student sign his or her name on the back. Then review fractions with the students. Finally, have the students divide their pizzas into six or eight equal pieces, using rulers and markers to draw the lines. Allow time for students to "share" their pizza with friends, finding someone to sign each slice.

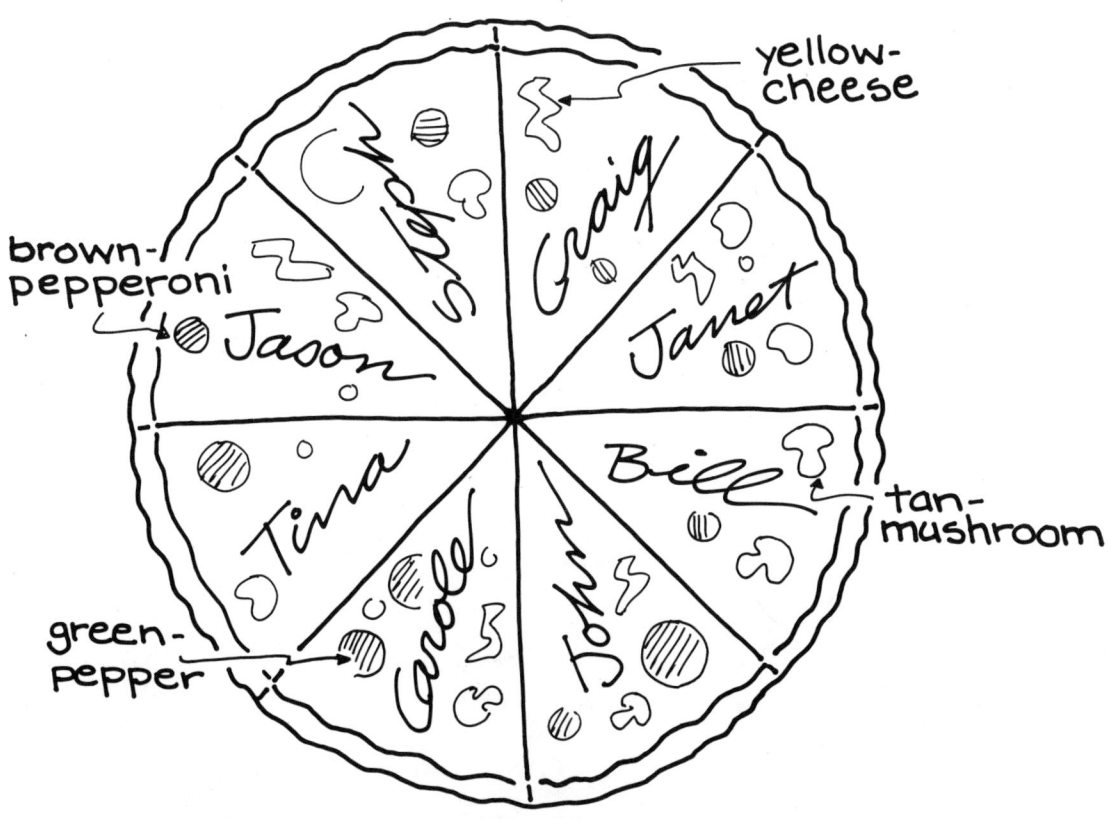

SEND WORD HOME

Students' writing shows what they have learned about a region.

MATERIALS:
Maps, travel brochures, 3" x 5" index cards, pens, markers, post cards (optional)

DIRECTIONS:
Set up a review center where students will demonstrate what they have learned about a region at the end of a social studies unit. Provide maps, travel brochures, index cards, pens, and markers. Display examples of real or made-up picture post cards from the region that was studied. On one side of the index cards, have students design their own picture post cards of the region. On the other side, children should write a message as though they were visiting the area and writing their classmates to tell about it. Display the post cards in the center for all the children to read.

CHAPTER 6
Thinking Games

VERBS GALORE

Students generate lists of verbs related to common objects.

MATERIALS:
Six to ten different common objects, paper, pencils

DIRECTIONS:
Divide the students into small groups of three or four. Give each group a different object, such as a ball, a toy car, a pencil, a light bulb, a clock, an eraser, a book. Ask each group to appoint one student to be the recorder for the group. Then, for ten minutes, have group members brainstorm as many verbs as they can associate with their object. The recorder's job is to list all verbs the group members say. The group with the ball, for example, might generate a list that includes throw, hit, go, fly, swing, crash, kick. At the end of the time, have the groups pass their objects on, change recorders, and follow the same procedure as before. Later, groups can share their objects and lists with the entire class. After the activity, objects and lists can be displayed and added to, if desired.

CONVERSATIONS

Children create a conversation with a book's main character.

MATERIALS:
A children's book, a stuffed animal or doll

DIRECTIONS:
Choose a children's book for which you have a stuffed animal to represent the main character. (Examples: a bear for *Corduroy*, a doll for *Goldilocks and the Three Bears*, or a toy monster for *Where The Wild Things Are*.) Read the book to the children and then introduce the stuffed animal or doll. Choose one student to sit in front of the character. Ask the student to help you by having a conversation with the character. Some coaching may be necessary, for example, you might say, "What would you like to know about Corduroy's day?" or "Is there something you would like to ask Goldilocks?" Take the character's part in the conversation yourself, answering the child. Encourage the children who are listening to make suggestions about the topics for the conversation. Add ideas and events from the story to the discussion.

VARIATION:
Older children can create imaginary conversations between two unlikely objects, for example, a globe and a tomato, a computer and a plant, an umbrella and a soccer ball. Set the two objects in the front of the room and ask for student volunteers to make up the conversations.

MAKING CONNECTIONS

Students figure out what trios of words have in common.

MATERIALS:
Chalkboard, chalk, paper, pencils

DIRECTIONS:
Write on the board the three words in one of the examples below. Help the students figure out what the three words have in common. Then write the rest of the examples on the board. Have students work in pairs to find the connection that links each trio of words. If time permits, allow the students to create their own word connections and have pairs present their three words to the class. Can the class discover the connection?

    Examples: back, saw, sea (horse)
                 board, hole, house (key)
                 rain, over, hanger (coat)
                 new, blue, shine (moon)
                 big, locker, ball (foot)
                 club, tree, sit (house)

MONDAY MEMORIES

Students associate descriptive words with their classmates and exercise their memories.

MATERIALS:
Chalkboard, chalk, chalk eraser, paper, pencils

DIRECTIONS:
On Monday mornings, ask each child to give you the two words that best describe his or her weekend. Have each one take a turn telling the words and explaining why they were chosen. For example, Jenny might say "popcorn" and "soccer" to indicate that over the weekend she ate popcorn while watching a movie with her sister and later played a game of soccer. As each student gives the words and explanations, write the two words on the chalkboard along with the student's name.

After all have taken a turn, go down the list of words. Use each pair to describe a totally new, but not necessarily realistic, activity. For example, you might say that Jenny had fun on the weekend by playing soccer with a popcorn ball. Encourage the children to make their own whimsical associations with the pairs of words. After you have reviewed the whole list, list the word pairs on a piece of paper and erase them from the board. Duplicate the list and, near the end of the day, give a copy to each child. Have the students try to remember which words were said by which classmates. Those who correctly remember the most win the game. For variety, have pairs of children work together and give Memory Game certificates to the pairs who correctly remember at least a certain number.

```
Grandma, K-Mart — Chris
park, squirrel — Sylvia
pizza, painting — Connie
firewood, marshmallows — Jim
library, birthday party — Gary
shoes, accident — Rachel
```

THE GREAT DIVIDE

This activity encourages students to look for commonalities and differences.

DIRECTIONS:
Decide on a particular criteria for dividing the children into two groups. For example:
- solid and patterned clothing
- tie shoes and non-tie shoes
- dark hair and light hair
- blue eyes and brown eyes
- children with freckles and those without
- children missing a front tooth and those with both front teeth
- children who ride the bus and those who walk

Then, with no explanation, begin to divide the students into two groups by calling one name at a time and pointing to the group the student should join. After you have chosen several children to join each of the two groups, say to the class, "Can anyone see how I decide in which group you belong?" Allow the children to guess while you continue dividing. After someone guesses the criteria correctly, allow the children who are not in a group to decide for themselves which group they should join.

VOCABULARY HELPER

A vocabulary chart helps students expand their knowledge of words.

MATERIALS:
Vocabulary chart pattern, dictionaries, pencils

DIRECTIONS:
Make copies of the vocabulary chart pattern for the class. Give a copy to each student and divide the students into groups of four. Have each student in a group choose a different new vocabulary word to work on. Then have the students fill out the vocabulary chart, starting with the new word. Provide dictionaries for students who need them. When the charts are completed, have students within a group share their charts with the other members.

VOCABULARY CHART

The word:	A sentence using the word:
A synonym for the word:	A picture that shows the meaning of the word:
An antonym of the word:	Number of syllables in the word:

GLOB IT UP

This game lets children practice using an unfamiliar word in sentences.

MATERIALS:
Chalkboard, chalk

DIRECTIONS:
Make up three sentences that include a new word, substituting the word "glob" for the word. For example:
   I used to go to Grandma's glob, but I don't go as much now.
   I glob eat ice cream for dessert.
   My mom's car breaks down glob.
After saying the three sentences, ask the class if anyone knows the word. When the word is guessed correctly, print it on the board. Ask a student to think of a new sentence with the word in it. Continue the game with more sentences made up for other new words.

VARIATION:
Make up similar sentences, one for each new word on a spelling or vocabulary list. Give a copy to each student and have students figure out which word on the list fits each sentence.

CHAPTER 7
Cabin Fever Games

GUESS WHO'S MISSING

Children figure out which classmate is hiding in this memory game.

DIRECTIONS:
Select a place in the room to be the designated hiding place during the game. Choose one child to be "It" and ask that child to leave the room. Of the children remaining, choose one child to hide in the designated hiding place. Have all the other children change seats. Then ask a child to act as the timekeeper. The timekeeper will watch the second hand of the clock and tell when one minute has passed. Have "It" return to the room and ask the timekeeper to begin timing one minute. "It" should then try to guess who is missing. If the missing child has not been identified when the time is up, he or she becomes the next child to leave the room. If the missing child is guessed within one minute, "It" gets another turn. Choose a new timekeeper for each round.

FOUR CORNERS

Sharp ears help in this elimination game.

MATERIALS:
Blindfold, four 10" x 10" cards, marker, tape

DIRECTIONS:
Label the four corners of the classroom with numbers from one to four. Choose one child to be "It" and place a blindfold over his or her eyes. Next, have "It" begin slowly counting aloud to ten. While "It" is counting, each child in the room should move to any one of the four corners. When ten is reached, "It" names a corner and says, for example, "Everyone in Corner Three should sit down." The children who were standing in Corner Three must take their seats. "It" begins counting to ten as before, and the remaining children choose a corner to stand in. "It" names a corner as before, and the game continues until only one child is left. That child becomes "It" for the next game.

VARIATION:
For older children, give the four corners their correct directional labels: north, south, east, and west, or northeast, northwest, southeast, and southwest.

GET IT TOGETHER

Children sort themselves into groups by choosing a category item.

MATERIALS:
Chalkboard, chalk

DIRECTIONS:
Write a category on the chalkboard and ask the children to name four items that belong in it. For example, if the category is fruit, the items might be apple, orange, banana, and apricot. Ask that each child pick one of the four items without telling anyone of the choice. Give a signal for the children to stand and find their group by saying the name of the item they picked over and over. When two children discover they're saying the same name, have them pair up. Then they should continue saying the name in unison and look for other group members. After four groups are formed, ask the group members to tell why they picked their particular item. Show the sizes of the groups with a graph on the chalkboard.

VARIATION:
Write four math problems on the board without the answers. Have the children choose one of the four problems and say the answer until they have formed four groups.

NURSERY RHYME MATCH-UP

Similar to Get It Together, this game has a different twist.

MATERIALS:
Scissors, paper, marker

DIRECTIONS:
Print a short nursery rhyme, poem, or song on a sheet of paper. Duplicate the page and cut it into strips with one line on each strip. Distribute one strip to each child. Tell the children they will find others who have the same line by standing and repeating their line. After the children have formed groups, do a complete reading of the nursery rhyme, starting with the group that has the first line. A sample nursery rhyme to use might be:
    Jack and Jill went up the hill
    To fetch a pail of water.
    Jack fell down and broke his crown
    And Jill came tumbling after.

VARIATION:
Choose a poem from your reading book or a song the children are learning in music class.

ADDITION RELAY

Teams race to add columns of numerals.

MATERIALS:
Chalkboard, chalk

DIRECTIONS:
Divide the children into two teams of equal size and have the teams line up at equal distances from the chalkboard. Have the first player from each team go to the chalkboard and write one numeral. Continue with each player, in turn, adding a number below his or her teammate's to form a column. The last player totals the column. Check the calculations and determine the winner. If one team did not add correctly, the other team is the winner. If both teams worked their problems correctly, the team that finished first is the winner.

DRAWING RELAY

Pictures drawn by team members must fit a theme.

MATERIALS:
Ten or fifteen small paper sheets, marker, shoebox, chalkboard, chalk

DIRECTIONS:
On each of 10 or 15 sheets of paper, write a theme or category. Place the sheets in a shoebox. Divide the class into two to four teams of equal size and have the teams line up, relay style, at equal distances from the chalkboard. Have the first player from each team draw a sheet of paper from the box and look at the theme or category. Then have him or her pass the sheet to the next player in line and go to the board to draw a simple picture that fits the theme. The next player should add another drawing, fitting the theme, and the relay should continue until all members of one team have drawn their pictures on the board. At that point, decide if all the team's drawings fit the theme and, if they do, the team wins. Some themes and categories might be:
  President's Day
  Valentine's Day
  St. Patrick's Day
  Things found in a refrigerator
  Things found at the beach
  Things found in a laboratory
  Things found in a garden
  Things found in a doctor's office

VARIATION:
Allow each team to choose its own theme and have players draw pictures that fit it.

MOVING NORTH

Children gain skills in applying the four basic compass directions.

DIRECTIONS:
Begin the game by reviewing the cardinal directions: north, south, east, and west. Point in each direction as you name it. Then give the children a command using one of the directions, for example, "Move one seat to the north." All of the children must change their seats as directed, but some children may have no seats to go to. In the example given, those children would take one step away from their seats, toward the north. Continue giving commands using the directions—"Move one seat to the east. Move two seats south. Move two seats west." Try to end up with the children seated at their original places.

BEANBAG DROP

Relay team members pass a beanbag down the line.

MATERIALS:
Two beanbags

DIRECTIONS:
Divide the children into two equal relay teams. Provide a beanbag for each team. Have the two teams line up and stand, one behind the other, facing the front. At the start signal, have the first child pass the beanbag to the teammate behind by raising it over his or her head and dropping it. The child standing behind must catch the beanbag as it is dropped, raise it over his or her head, and drop it to the next child. The last child in the team should run to the front of the line and drop the beanbag on the floor. If a team member fails to catch the beanbag, it goes back to the front of the line and the team must start over. The first team to complete the sequence wins the race.

WORLD TRAVELER

Students use a globe to trace a route between two countries.

MATERIALS:
Globe, 40 to 50 index cards, marker, grocery bag, small post-it notes, paper and pencils (optional)

DIRECTIONS:
On each index card, write the name of one of the nations shown on the globe. Place all the cards in the grocery bag. Then demonstrate the activity to the class. Without looking, draw two cards from the bag. Place a small post-it note on the globe over each nation named on the cards. Trace with your finger a straight line on the globe between the two nations. As your finger "travels," name every country and body of water that it passes over. After the demonstration, place the materials at a table and have small groups of students do the activity. One child might record the countries and oceans as another calls them out.

SIGNS ON STUDENTS

Students make and wear signs that tell about themselves.

MATERIALS:
Paper, pencils, tape

DIRECTIONS:
Ask students to take out a piece of paper. Then ask them to do the following:
1. Write your name in the middle of the paper.
2. Below your name, write the name of your favorite song.
3. Above your name, write the name of your favorite book.
4. In one corner, write what you think when you hear the word "learn."
5. In another corner, write what you think when you hear the word "friend."
6. Wherever you can, write what you think when you hear the word "math."

Have the students tape their papers on themselves. Then have them share their papers with each other by walking around the classroom and reading each other's information. Ask the students to read in silence, so that they can concentrate on what each has written. Then, hold a discussion about what the students have learned.

PART III
Ending with a Bang

CHAPTER 8

Special Interest Days

DAD'S DOUGHNUT DAY

Special breakfast-time activities can involve the fathers of children in your own class or in the whole school.

Doughnut Day Name Tags and Invitations

MATERIALS:
Construction paper in various colors, pencils, scissors, hole punch, glue, markers, pins, cake decorations (optional)

DIRECTIONS:
Outline on construction paper enough doughnuts for all the children and their dads. Cut out the doughnuts and allow the children to decorate their doughnut name tags by gluing on cake decorations or colorful dots cut with a hole punch. Use a marker to print the name on each name tag. To make the invitations, outline the pattern and cut on the fold of the construction paper. Have the children decorate the front of the invitations as they did the name tags. Inside, the children can copy the invitation you write. For example,

    Dad, you are invited
    To Dad's Doughnut Day
    at Greenwood Elementary School
    February 16, 199-
    7:30 - 8:30 a.m.

Send the invitations home a week in advance.

NOTE: If a dad is not available, students might invite other relatives or adult friends.

Doughnut Day Refreshments

MATERIALS:
Serving table, tablecloth, cups, napkins, doughnuts, apple juice

DIRECTIONS:
Allow the children to set up the serving table with the tablecloth, cups, and napkins. Place the doughnuts and apple juice on the table and arrange the doughnut name tags. As the fathers come in, have the children act as hosts and hostesses. Each child should serve his or her father a doughnut and some juice.

Invent a Doughnut

MATERIALS:
Paper, pencils or markers

DIRECTIONS:
Ask the dads and children to list as many kinds of doughnuts as they can. Then ask each dad and child to invent a new kind of doughnut. Provide paper and pencils for drawing the doughnut inventions and allow each team to present its invention for the others to see.

Doughnut Circumference

MATERIALS:
Doughnuts, string, rulers, paper, pencils or markers, construction paper, pushpins

DIRECTIONS:
With their dads, have the children measure the circumference of a doughnut with string and a ruler. Challenge each pair to find something in the room that has the same circumference. Provide paper so that each team can draw a diagram of the doughnut and the same-circumference object they found. Mount the diagrams on a bulletin board under the caption WHAT'S AS ROUND AS A DOUGHNUT?

Doughnut Estimations

MATERIALS:
Paper, pencils, doughnuts, waxed paper, scale, chalkboard, chalk

DIRECTIONS:
Ask each dad-and-child team to estimate how many doughnuts it would take to make a pound. Have each team write its prediction on a piece of paper and sign their names. Collect the predictions from the teams. Use a scale that will show one pound, covering the surface with waxed paper. Put one doughnut at a time on the scale until the weight equals one pound. Allow the children to count aloud as each doughnut is placed on the scale. Write the number of doughnuts on the chalkboard. Then check the predictions to see which team or child came closest to the correct number.

The Doughnut Hole

MATERIALS:
Paper, pencils, chart paper, marker

DIRECTIONS:
After the dads have gone, ask the children to tell why they think there is no center in a doughnut. Encourage creative answers. Then have the children write a paragraph on their own paper where they think the doughnut hole is. Ask the children to form four-member teams and share their answers. Have each group discuss the best answers and choose one to represent their group. As the answers are shared, print them on chart paper under the caption WHAT HAPPENED TO THE DOUGHNUT HOLE?

RAINBOW WEEK

The following activities will help promote self-esteem.

Parent Letter

MATERIALS:
Copies of the letter to parents

DIRECTIONS:
Copy the following letter for each child and send it home to parents:

Dear Parents,
    Next week our class [or school] will celebrate a special week that we call Rainbow Week. Just as each rainbow that appears in the sky is different and unique, so is your child. We think a whole week to celebrate our specialness is worth your knowing about. But we need your help to make this week even more fun and special. Each day next week will have a color. We will all wear that color to remind each of us that it is Rainbow Week. Please help your child find something to wear each day that's the color I've listed below:
    Monday - red
    Tuesday - blue
    Wednesday - green
    Thursday - yellow
    Friday - orange
Thank you for helping us celebrate Rainbow Week!
                      Yours truly,

Door Banners

MATERIALS:
Pencils, construction paper, scissors, markers, yarn, hole punch

DIRECTIONS:
List the name of the principal, teachers, secretary, custodians, and other support staff. Cut a door banner for each person on the list. Have each child choose a name from the list and take a door banner to decorate. Encourage the children to write a short message on the banner to show the person that he or she is appreciated. For example, "Miss Grayer, you are the greatest!" "Mr. Jacobs, we think you are special." Then punch holes at the top of each banner and tie a length of yarn through the holes. Allow each child to hang the door banner in the appropriate room.

Secret Buddy/Heart Friend

MATERIALS:
Slips of paper, hat, marker

DIRECTIONS:
Write each student's name on a slip of paper and place all the slips in a hat. Have students draw a name out of the hat and ask each of them to plan a nice surprise for the selected person during that week. The surprise might be a small treat or toy, a note of appreciation, a made-up award, or a handmade book of riddles or cartoons. Tell the children to place the surprise on the student's desk without him or her knowing. At the end of the week, let students discover who their secret buddies or heart friends were.

Our Golden Deeds

MATERIALS:
Gold, black, and other colors of construction paper, scissors, stapler

DIRECTIONS:
Make a big kettle out of the black construction paper and mount it on the bulletin board as shown in the illustration. Cut letters for the bulletin board title OUR GOLDEN DEEDS and staple them above the kettle. Then cut 100 to 150 large coins from the gold paper and provide each child with a supply. Tell the children that they should watch for times when they see a classmate doing something helpful or nice for someone else and, without telling anyone, write the child's name on a gold coin. Older children can also write a sentence to tell what they saw the child doing. Staple the coins on the bulletin board on the black pot of gold. At the end of each day of Rainbow Week, read aloud the names on the coins.

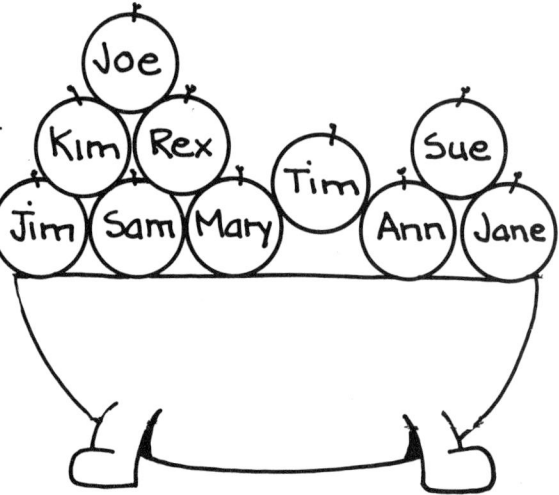

Rainbow Treats

MATERIALS:
Fruit juices, Styrofoam cups, Popsicle sticks

DIRECTIONS:
Make rainbow popsicles with fruit juices that match the day's color: cranberry or mixed fruit juice for red day, grape juice for blue day, pineapple juice for yellow day, orange juice for orange day, and apple juice with green food coloring for green day. Freeze the juice in Styrofoam cups with a Popsicle stick. Serve the treats for a snack on the appropriate day.

GUESSTIMATION DAY

This day will help children see all the ways to make estimations.

Guesstimation Game

MATERIALS:
Baby food jars, paper, pencils

DIRECTIONS:
Send a baby food jar home with each child. Explain to the children that at home they should each find something small—cereal, rice, macaroni, pebbles, Styrofoam peanuts, or the like—to fill the jar with. Have them count the items they put in, but not tell any classmate the number. The next day, set up an estimation center at a desk in the room. Have each child put his or her jar on a sheet of paper. Children should write their names at the top of their papers. As they have time during the day, allow children to go to the estimation center and guess how many items are in the jars. Have them write their estimation on each sheet, along with their name. At the end of the day, have each child collect his or her own jar and the paper with the estimations. Ask the children to determine who came the closest to the actual number of items in each jar and to announce the names to the class. The students should present the winners with the appropriate jars.

Investigation Teams

MATERIALS:
Six index cards, marker

DIRECTIONS:
Print one of the following questions on each of the index cards:
- How many cars are in the parking lot?
- How many cars will pass in front of the school in five minutes?
- How many doorknobs are in the school?
- How many hot lunches does the cafeteria serve in one day?
- How many times does the secretary's phone ring in 15 minutes?
- How many bulletin boards are in the halls of the school?

Divide the children into six investigation teams. Give each team an index card with a problem on it and ask the teams to consider the following questions before they solve their problem:
- What is one way to figure out the answer without counting?
- What would be a reasonable answer?
- What do we already know that would help us solve the problem?

Allow the teams 15 minutes to discuss the problem. When the discussion is over, ask the teams to predict the answer to their problem and to be prepared to share the problem and prediction with the class. Then have each team find the solution to its problem and present the solution to the class.

PERSONALIZED LEARNING DAY

Assemble special resources for learning geared to individual interests.

MATERIALS:
Copies of the interest survey, resource materials

DIRECTIONS:
Make copies of the interest survey and pass them out to the children. After everyone has completed a survey, collect the papers and compile the results. Try to identify eight to ten topics that would appeal to most or all of the children and arrange to have special resources for them available on a certain day. For example, you could invite guest speakers to come to visit the class that day and ask the school librarian to help you gather relevant library books, films, and tapes. Have the class write letters to gather information from such sources as the National Wildlife Federation, National Park Service, Bureau of Outdoor Recreation, or Water Resources Council.

INDIVIDUAL INTEREST SURVEY

1. The two things I like best at school are _____
_____.

2. The two things I like least at school are _____
_____.

3. Three things I would like to learn more about at school are _____
_____.

4. Three things I like to do best when I get home are _____
_____.

5. Three things I like to do least when I get home are _____
_____.

6. I like to read about_____
and_____.

7. I like to see movies and TV programs about_____
and_____.

8. I like to take trips to_____
_____.

9. When I grow up I want to be_____
_____.

10. I like to collect_____
_____.

11. The famous person I most admire is_____
_____.

12. My favorite animal is_____
_____.

13. One thing I've always wondered is_____
_____.

CHAPTER 9
The Great Outdoors

WALK A MILE

Children get "feet-on" experience with a one-mile distance.

MATERIALS:
Chart paper and markers, watch

DIRECTIONS:
Before the lesson, measure a mile by driving in your car to a point half a mile away from school and back. To demonstrate to the class how far a mile is, begin by asking students to show you something in their desks or in the room that is the same length as an inch, a foot, and a yard. Then ask them to describe how far a mile is. Ask the class to name some locations that they think are half a mile from school. Write each answer on chart paper along with the name of the child who suggested it. Then tell the students that you will show them how far a mile is. Take a walk following the route you measured with your car. Ask a child wearing a watch to time how long it takes to walk a mile. Stop along the way and ask the class, "Do you think we've walked a mile yet?" When you return to school, ask the students to look at the chart and check their predictions. Whose prediction was the most accurate?

ODD OR EVEN?

Teams compete to collect the most beans.

MATERIALS:
Two plastic buckets or bowls, a bag of dried beans

DIRECTIONS:
Whisper a number to each student and ask the student to decide if the number is odd or even. Students should not tell their numbers to anyone. Choose two students to be team leaders, one for the even numbers and one for the odd, and provide each with a plastic bowl or bucket. Have everyone go outside to a paved play area and watch you toss all of the dried beans onto the pavement. On a signal from you, have each student find a bean and stand on it. Then have each student signal to the team leaders by saying his or her number over and over until the correct team leader arrives. Have the leader pick up the bean the child is standing on. For example, a child with the number two says "two" until the even team leader picks up the bean. Set a time limit (15 minutes) for play. Then ask the team leaders to count the beans to determine the winning team. The team with the most beans wins.

FIREFIGHTER RELAYS

Teams pass a bucket of water from member to member.

MATERIALS:
Bucket for each team, water

DIRECTIONS:
Divide the students into two or three teams. Give each team a bucket with water in it. On your signal tell the teams to pass the bucket down their lines without spilling the water. After the last person runs the bucket to the front of the line, have the team pass it down the line again. Continue play until each child has had an opportunity to run the bucket to the start, and the team sits down to show it is finished. The first team to finish wins.

BALLOON FLOAT

Students try to keep balloons aloft as long as possible.

MATERIALS:
Markers, balloons in four colors

DIRECTIONS:
Print the initials of each student on a flat balloon and then distribute the balloons, dividing the colors equally. Have the students blow their balloons up. Divide the children into four teams, each with the same color balloons. On your signal have the students throw their balloons in the air and see who can keep the balloon in the air the longest. When a balloon touches the ground, that student should sit down. When all the balloons are down, ask each team to pick the three children who kept their balloons in the air the longest. Have those children see how long they can keep their balloons in the air a second time. After that round, ask each team to send in the one person from the team that they think can keep the balloon in the air the longest. Declare the winner of this final round the champion.

VARIATION:
Play the game in the same way, but with special restrictions: using only one hand, using only the non-dominant hand, or sitting down.

PEANUT PICK-UP

Players race for peanuts in this team game.

MATERIALS:
Cardboard box, Styrofoam peanuts

DIRECTIONS:
Place a box of Styrofoam peanuts between two equal teams lined up about 50 feet apart. Give each player on each team a number by counting consecutively from opposite ends of the teams. Choose one student to serve as the leader who will call the numbers and keep score. Begin the game by having the leader call a number. The two players with that number should race to the box, pick up one Styrofoam peanut each, and return to their places. The first player to return to the line earns one point for his or her team. After everyone's number has been called, the team with the most points wins. The leader may call a number twice, but every number must be called before the game is over and a winner declared. (To find out what numbers have been called, check which students have Styrofoam peanuts.)

SCATTER BALL

Teams try to score while defending their own goals.

MATERIALS:
Rubber ball, chalk or yarn, whistle

DIRECTIONS:
Mark or draw a goal line at each end of the play area. Divide the students into two teams and allow them to choose team names. Start the game by placing the ball in the center of the field. Have the players stand ten feet from the ball and run toward it after you or a team leader blow a whistle. The object of the game is for each team to get the ball across the opponent's goal line while defending its own goal line against scoring. Each team must defend its goal line with some of its players while others move the ball and try to score. A goal is scored by hitting, kicking, throwing, or rolling the ball across the opponent's goal line. Each time a team scores a goal it earns one point. Center the ball in the field each time a goal is scored.

FALL OUT

Children caught holding the ball must sit inside the circle.

MATERIALS:
Two rubber balls, whistle

DIRECTIONS:
Have the children stand in a circle with two players each holding a ball. Blow the whistle to start the children passing the balls. When you blow the whistle again, the two children holding the balls must drop out to sit inside the circle. Have the remaining children continue play until four children are left. Then remove one of the balls and resume play until one child is left. That child becomes the game leader for the next round of Fall Out.

THE SHOCKER

One child inside a circle tries to discern which player is squeezing another's hand.

DIRECTIONS:
Form a large circle with all the students except one holding hands. Have the remaining student stand in the circle's center and try to find "The Shocker"—the person who is squeezing another player's hand. Designate someone to start the shock without the child in the center knowing. The shock may move in either direction and may be sent back and forth but only one shock can occur in the circle at a time. If the shocker is caught, he or she takes the place of the child in the center.

CHAPTER 10
Parting Company

DINOSAUR EGG PICNIC

Plan a surprise picnic with parents or the school cafeteria staff.

MATERIALS:
Three or four watermelons, index cards, marker, paper plates, knife

DIRECTIONS:
Label three or four watermelons with the names of dinosaurs, for example: brontosaurus, stegosaurus, allosaurus, triceratops, tyrannosaurus rex. Ask a parent or school staff member to hide the watermelons in a neighborhood park or on the school grounds. Divide the children into three or four groups and explain that they are looking for their dinosaur's egg. Give each team a card that tells the name of the dinosaur whose egg they are looking for. Allow the children to look in the area until they find the egg and then have them bring it to a designated area. Keep acting as though each watermelon is an egg. When all of the teams have returned, break open the "eggs" and hand out slices of watermelon. Announce to the children that this special picnic has been planned to celebrate the end of the year.

PICNIC TREASURE HUNT

Upper-grade children will enjoy this new twist on lesson review.

MATERIALS:
Copies of one lesson review sheet, scissors, eight 12" x 12" poster board cards, markers, tape, award certificates

DIRECTIONS:
Plan this treasure hunt—with a surprise picnic at the end—with the help of parents or the cafeteria staff. Ahead of time, choose which lesson review sheet (on the following pages) you will use, or make up your own. Adapt the clue locations to fit your building. Make five copies of the review sheet, saving one to guide you in laying out the treasure hunt course. Cut the side strips from the other four copies and discard them. Then cut the copies apart into four clue strips. Mark four cards with this sign: Ø, and four cards with this sign: N/C (N/C = next clue, Ø = try again). Arrange for help with food and drinks on the day of the picnic treasure hunt. On the morning of the treasure hunt, lay out the course. Mount the appropriate sign at each location. At each N/C location, place the three clue strips that belong there (follow the order on your review sheet).

To start the treasure hunt, divide the children into four teams. Explain that the students will do a lesson review activity in the form of a treasure hunt. Have each team make up a team name. Then give each team a different clue strip and a marker and explain that teams should select an answer and go to the spot named. If they see a N/C sign, they should sign their team name on it and pick up the next clue. If they see a Ø, they should try the location for the other answer on their clue sheet. Instruct teams to go to a designated spot after they have signed their team name four times. After the teams have all gathered at that spot, announce that the "treasure" will be a picnic lunch. Ask a parent to collect the signs and show them to the teams. Award certificates to the team that finished first, the team that got lost the most, and the team with the most creative name.

106

ENGLISH LESSON REVIEW

N/C | If the name of our school is a proper noun, go to the secretary's desk.

Ø | If the name of our school is a common noun, go to the courtyard.

N/C | If ball/bawl is a homophone, go to the phone desk.

Ø | If ball/bawl is a homograph, go to the janitor's closet.

N/C | If ran is a verb in the past tense, go to the running track.

Ø | If running is a verb in the future tense, go to the basketball goal.

N/C | If the sentence "The cat and dog were fighting" has a compound subject, go to the kindergarten door.

Ø | If the sentence "The cat and dog were fighting" has a compound predicate, go to the four-square area.

SOCIAL STUDIES LESSON REVIEW

N/C | If a peninsula is surrounded by water on three sides, go to the primary swing sets.

Ø | If a peninsula is completely surrounded by water, go to the nurse's office.

N/C | If a mesa has a flat top and straight sides, go to the flagpole.

Ø | If a mesa has a peaked top and sloping sides, go to the P.E. storage closet.

N/C | If the source of a river is where a river begins, go to the front door.

Ø | If the mouth of a river is where a river begins, go to the front chalkboard.

N/C | If a tributary runs into a larger river, go to the milk cooler.

Ø | If a tributary runs out of a larger river, go to the PTA desk.

MATH LESSON REVIEW

N/C | If the correct way to find the perimeter of your backyard is to add all the dimensions together, go to the principal's office.

Ø | If the correct way to find the perimeter of your backyard is to multiply length times width, go to the nurse's office.

N/C | If the correct way to find the area of your room is to multiply length times width, go to the south kindergarten room.

Ø | If the correct way to find the area of your room is to add the length and width, go to the first grade room.

N/C | If a hexagon has six sides, go to the north bench.

Ø | If a hexagon has five sides, go to the south bench.

N/C | If an octagon has eight sides, go to the basketball goal.

Ø | If an octagon has nine sides, go to the jungle gym.

EXPOSITION DAY

This event enables children to share their school accomplishments.

MATERIALS:
Paper, pencils (other materials will vary)

DIRECTIONS:
Work with several teachers or the whole school to provide the children with an opportunity to share information about their successes during the school year. Start by asking students to each list two or three things they feel they were successful with, for example: the science fair, math problems, spelling tests, gym games. Group children into teams according to their accomplishments. For example, team together children who felt they were successful with computers and form another group of children who were pleased with their artwork. Ask members of each team to think of a way they could demonstrate their successes to children from other grades, for example: through a poster, a collage of their best work, or a live commercial about their work. Allow time for the teams to plan their presentations. Toward the end of the year, set aside a day for students to visit other classrooms and share demonstrations.

YOUR AFTERNOON PLAN

Children make individual plans for themselves for an afternoon at school.

MATERIALS:
Chalkboard, chalk, paper, pencils, tape

DIRECTIONS:
Toward the end of the school year, announce to the students that each of them will be in charge of making an individual plan for himself or herself for one afternoon of a school day. Explain that you will give the students guidelines to follow and that their written plans must be approved by you. As a class, brainstorm ideas for activities that would be appropriate for that afternoon, for example: draw on art paper, read a book, clean out my desk, play a game with a friend. Write all of the options on the chalkboard. Allow time for the children to make their plans, complete with the time scheduled for each activity. As they finish, have the students come to you for approval. Announce the day that the plans will be carried out. On that day, after lunch, ask each child to post his or her plan, taping it on the side or front of the desk. At the end of the afternoon, lead a discussion about how the afternoon went. Discuss what it felt like to make their own plans and whether it was difficult for them.

IT'S THE LAST DAY!

Try these activities on the last day of school.

Graffiti Board

MATERIALS:
Kraft paper, markers, crayons

DIRECTIONS:
When you take down the bulletin board display at the end of the school year, put up kraft paper and allow the children to write good graffiti on it. Explain the rules for good graffiti:
- Say only nice things about yourself or others.
- Use language that is suitable for school.
- Draw pictures that are suitable for school.

Bumper Stickers

MATERIALS:
Solid-colored contact paper, permanent markers, scissors

DIRECTIONS:
Cut a number of rectangles from contact paper. Then ask each child to make a bumper sticker to celebrate his or her promotion to the next grade. Have the children use the markers to decorate and write on the stickers. Just before they leave school on the last day, invite the children to wear their bumper stickers "on their bumpers."